Finding My Father's Auschwitz File

Allen Hershkowitz

Chapbook Press

Schuler Books
2660 28th Street SE
Grand Rapids, MI 49512
(616) 942-7330
www.schulerbooks.com

Finding My Father's Auschwitz File

ISBN: 9781957169781

eBook ISBN: 9781957169798

Library of Congress Control Number: 2024906269

Printed in the United States.

Dedicated to Dylan, Lea, Connor, Michael, Suzanne,
Dale and all Hershkowitz family members
who follow.

~

Konzentrationslager Auschwitz Art der Haft: Sch. Jude Gef. Nr. 124124

Name und Vorname: HERSZKOWICZ LAJZER ISRAEL

geb.: 12.12.08 zu: Lubien Kr. Leslau

Wohnort: Lubien, Kr. Leslau, Warthegau

Beruf: Arbeiter Rel.: mos.

Staatsangehörigkeit: ehem. Polen Stand: verh.

Name der Eltern: Jojna, Ryfka geb. Krejnik Rasse: jüd.

Wohnort: unb Adr.

Name der Ehefrau: Cypre geb. Swocra Rasse: jüd.

Wohnort: unb Adr. Beine n. Ang.

Kinder: 2 Alleiniger Ernährer der Familie oder der Eltern: nein

Vorbildung: 4 Kl. Volkss.

Militärdienstzeit: von — bis

Kriegsdienstzeit: von — bis

Grösse: 167 Nase: gross Haare: braun Gestalt: schlank

Mund: norm. Bart: keinen Gesicht: oval Ohren: n. anl.

Sprache: poln. deutsch Augen: braun Zähne: seh 24

Ansteckende Krankheiten oder Gebrechen: keine

Besondere Kennzeichen: keine

Rentenempfänger: nein

Verhaftet am: 1941 1943 Lubien

1. Mal eingelief.: 2. Mal eingeliefert

Einweisende Dienststelle: RSHA, IV B4a 2023/43 (331)

Grund:

Parteizugehörigkeit: keine von—bis

Welche Funktionen: keine

Mitglied v. Unterorganisationen: nein

Kriminelle Vorstrafen: o. Ang. keine

Politische Vorstrafen: o. ang. keine

Ich bin darauf hingewiesen worden, dass meine Bestrafung wegen intellektueller Urkundenfälschung erfolgt, wenn sich die obigen Angaben als falsch erweisen sollten.

v. g. u.   Der Lagerkommandant KL.-Au.
                                                i. A.

Lajzer Herszkowicz
12/12 1908

Auschwitz Induction Form for Leon Hershkowitz Filled Out By Nazi Agent Upon Leon's Arrival at the Death Camp on June 6, 1943. Very few of these forms survived the Nazi's destruction of death camp records. It is among the rarest artifacts of the Holocaust

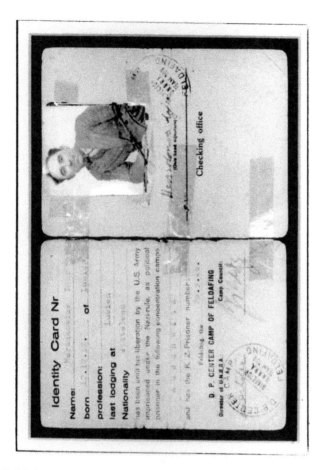

Feldafing Displaced Persons (DP) Camp ID Card of Leon Hershkowitz. After surviving prison, Auschwitz, the Death March, Gros Rosen and Dachau, Leon was sent to Feldafing after the war ended. This is where he met Helen, his future wife. Note the reference to his nationality being "Stateless" and his classification as a "Political Prisoner."

On October 3rd 2011 at 8:30 AM, during the High Holy Days of the Jewish New Year, I walked into Block 24 at the Auschwitz concentration camp in Oswiecim, Poland. The High Holy Days, the "Days of Awe," is the time of year when Jews contemplate our morality and our mortality, the meaning of our past, our place in the world, and our hopes for the future. It is a time we pray to be written into the Book of Life, asking for another year from the Almighty. It is a time we pray for the souls of our ancestors and for the future of our children. It is a time of repentance and, during the ten days between Rosh ha-Shanah and Yom Kippur, a time of almost unending contemplation and prayer. It is the most sacred, holy and thoughtful time of the year. A time we ask for our lives to be renewed. In 2011, I chose to spend two of those days at Auschwitz.

Block 24, a former prisoner barrack, rectangular, with a pitch roof, is constructed of red brick. Unlike the majority of barracks at the Auschwitz-Birkeneau concentration camp, which were built of wood and are now all gone due to decay, Block 24 still stands, a brick remnant of the Polish military base located at that site before World War II, before the Nazis took over the facility and turned it into the most notorious death camp the world has ever known.

The Auschwitz-Birkeneau concentration camp is now a state run museum and Block 24 hosts the camp's archivists' office. Prior to my arrival, the last member of my family I know of to walk these grounds was my father, Leon Hershkowitz, when he was a prisoner in this death camp. If other ancestors of mine were imprisoned in Auschwitz during the Nazis' war against the Jews, I do not know. Every Yom Kippur in my boyhood home, before reciting Kaddish for the dead, my mother—Helen Hershkowitz--lit twenty-two yahrzeit candles in memory of my parents' children, as well as my parents' parents, brothers, sisters, nieces, and nephews who were murdered by the Nazis. Who among those family members perished at Auschwitz I do not know. My father's first wife and two sons were murdered before he was sent to Auschwitz, and my mother's first husband and daughter were murdered also, most likely in the Stutthof or the Dachau concentration camp, the two death camps in which she spent virtually the entire war.

I was acutely aware of the contrast between my father's forced incarceration at Auschwitz and my voluntary visit. In contrast to the filthy, flimsy and cardboard-stiff striped prisoner uniform my father wore there, I was wearing a freshly pressed and finely tailored blue wool suit, a soft cotton light blue shirt and a blue silk tie. My father's shoes at Auschwitz, taken from the feet of dead or dying prisoners during his incarceration, were misshapen, mismatched, uncomfortable and wooden. My shoes, of comfortable Italian leather, were purchased in Milan. My father could not openly practice his religion at the camp, so I carried his white and black talis—prayer shawl—in its velvet case. His talis is now old and yellowing, narrow, smallish, with knotted fringes. It seems so much smaller to me now than when I was a boy and I watched him cover his shoulders with it in the synagogue or when he prayed at home. I wore a blue velvet yarmulke with silver yarn trimming. It was from my bar mitzvah, which took place on April 27, 1968, more than forty-three years before my visit.

This was my first trip to Auschwitz. I had planned to visit a number of times in the past, hoping to take my three children with me, but I could never seem to work out the logistics. More likely, I was reluctant to bring my children there: Over the years I had no trouble working out the logistics of taking them out west, to Alaska, China, Japan, Brazil, Sweden, France and so many other places, but somehow I couldn't bring myself to arrange a family visit to Poland, the country where both my parents were born. Auschwitz was not a destination I was emotionally able to bring my children to visit.

With the hundredth anniversary of my father's birth approaching--he was born December 12, 1912--I decided it was time for me to visit the camp, with or without them. My work as a Senior Scientist at the Natural Resources Defense Council — an environmental research and advocacy group -- often took me to Europe, so after delivering a speech in Portugal in September, 2011, I took a detour on my way home for the High Holy Days and finally visited

Auschwitz. On three previous occasions I had visited the Dachau concentration camp outside of Munich, where my mother was imprisoned.

Auschwitz and the Dachau concentration camp frame the emotional structure of my life. Thinking of my father in the course of a day I think of Auschwitz. Thinking about my mother, I think about Dachau. I still think often about their murdered children and murdered spouses. When I was younger I would think of Nazis when I exercised, building up my strength for my own anticipated confrontation. Last week I dreamt that Nazis were in my home, gassing me to death in my bedroom. When I opened my bathroom window to escape, they were waiting for me in the woods behind my home. I don't dream of Nazis every night, but I dream of them too much. Because the Holocaust is so ingrained in my soul I cannot bear to watch films about it.

The few details I know about my parents' day-to-day existence in Auschwitz and Dachau are drawn from the few memories my parents shared. I knew there was much I didn't learn from them about their past, but it was not until I discovered my father's

Auschwitz file that I recognized how far from understanding their history I was.

Until I was well into my teens, the only friends my parents had were other survivors of concentration camps. More than a dozen survivors would gather in my home on Saturday nights to play cards and share stories, except when I walked into the room, when they would fall silent. They called themselves "The Herring Club," because herring would be served at each gathering. Of course, they spoke only Yiddish, which was my first language. Among them there was Mira Salberg, a tall seamstress who made my sister's skirts for school, and her pint-sized husband Mendel, who also worked in the garment industry. There was Roman Goldberg, who we called "Rumick," an egomaniacal and always well-groomed locksmith, and his diminutive wife Lola, my mother's best friend—and my favorite--who fed me lunch for years when I was a boy in elementary school because my mother was usually at work. There was Sara Lensen, another seamstress, missing half of her jaw to cancer, who made the pillows for a couch I built from scrap wood for my first apartment when I was in college. Sara was married to Schmuel, a rotund man who said little but ate a lot. I recall how surprised I was to learn in elementary school that some of my Jewish friends had parents who were not concentration camp survivors. I felt similarly surprised to learn that there were Jews who did not speak Yiddish. To say my parents kept me sheltered as a child would be a great understatement. But it is understandable: having three murdered children between them, my parents chose to keep me close to home—very close.

Based on regular exposure to my parents' friends, and my regular interaction with their children, I deduced that Holocaust survivors tend to fall into two categories when it comes to recounting their wartime experiences: One group, seeking to ensure that the world would "Never Forget," spoke often to their children about their imprisonment, telling them everything they could remember. The second group, perhaps too traumatized to recount the horror they endured, perhaps seeking to protect their children's innocent minds, perhaps simply focused on building a new life, told their children very little. My parents were in this second category. As a consequence, my sister, (five years older than me), and I learned very little about our parents' history when we were growing up. I picked up bits and pieces about their origins from fragments they infrequently uttered, or from the two or three relatives who also survived WW II, or from the child of another more talkative survivor in whom my mother or father had confided during their Herring Club games. As a boy, I envied the children whose parents told them everything: They knew where their parents were from. I didn't. They knew something about their grandparents, their aunts and uncles. I was never told why I had none. They understood more about why our parents cried so often, and I knew almost nothing, though I seemed to feel everything. I felt their sadness and their fear. I felt their sense of vulnerability. We were not under enemy attack, but I nevertheless felt that the world could turn upside-down at any moment. My mother told me often to trust no one and reminded me equally often that only an education cannot be confiscated. As a boy, I was never harassed but I nevertheless came to expect that anything I had might at any minute be taken away, except what I picked up in books. I learned to anticipate that the more happy the holiday, the sadder and more silent my parents would become. There were just too many family members missing.

Including their three murdered children. But as I grew older I watched the children of the talkative survivors struggle with the emotional scars that come with learning too much at a young age about murdered relatives, death camps, torture, thievery and other Nazi atrocities. While it was frustrating as a boy to be kept in the dark, now, as a man, I am thankful that it took many more years for me to learn the details of what those children had learned at too young an age.

On October 2nd, the day before I entered Block 24, I had visited Auschwitz with a guide. Because I had told my guide that my father had been imprisoned at Auschwitz, at the end of the day she gave me a form from her car, told me to fill it out and said that when I came back the next day I should deliver it "to the office" in Block 24. Was the form I was to deliver going to lead to new information about my father's time here? Could a tangible historical record of his incarceration exist?

Among the short list of brief questions on the form was one titled simply "Camp Number in KL Auschwitz." (KL stands for Konzentrationslager, or concentration camp.) Of the 1.1 million Jews who were shipped to Auschwitz, about 200,000 were tattooed upon arrival with registration numbers. Another 200,000 non-Jews were also tattooed. I filled in the form with the "Camp Number" that was tattooed onto my father's left arm: 124124, a number etched into my soul for as long as I can remember. In front of the numbers on his arm was what looked to me to be a triangle. Much later in life I learned it was supposed to be an "A", which is how the Nazis signified that the recipient of the tattoo was a Jew.

According to the writer Primo Levi, whose incarceration at Auschwitz overlapped with the latter months of my father's more lengthy imprisonment, "The [tattooing] operation was slightly painful and extraordinarily rapid: they placed us all in a row, and one by one, according to the alphabetical order of our names, we filed past a skillful official, armed with a sort of pointed tool with a very short needle. It seems that this is the real, true initiation: only by 'showing one's number' can one get bread and soup...And for many days, while the habits of freedom still led me to look for the time on my wristwatch, my new name ironically appeared instead, a number tattooed in bluish characters under the skin."[1]

These 400,000 dehumanized, tattooed prisoners, my father among them, were actually among the "lucky" entrants; they were to become slave laborers: By contrast, 75 percent of Auschwitz entrants were arbitrarily selected to be killed upon their arrival. My father was among those who had the good fortune of being selected to be worked to death.

The interior walls of Block 24 are concrete painted light beige. Windowless steel doors run down the hallway. The doors were all closed when I arrived, so I opened the first one I came to.

The room I entered was the anteroom to the Auschwitz archivist's office. In the middle of the room was a large rectangular wooden table and some chairs. A window at the far end opened to the grounds of the camp. As I entered the room, I noticed that the wall on my **right** held a large glass window, perhaps four feet high by eight feet wide. Behind the window a woman sat at a desk typing.

She was young and attractive, perhaps in her mid-twenties with dark short-cropped hair. I tapped on the window. She looked up towards me, and indicated with her hand that I should wait.

As I waited I examined the room where the typist worked. It was long and rectangular, dominated by rows of large metal file cabinets, steel grey and perhaps six feet high. The cabinets filled the middle of the room, virtually from end to end and side to side, with about six feet of space surrounding the file cabinets on each side, for desks and chairs.

What is referred to as the Auschwitz concentration camp is actually a complex of three facilities. Auschwitz I was a penal colony. A former Polish military facility before the War, its barracks were built of brick and concrete. It is the entrance gate to Auschwitz I, (and also the entrance gate to Dachau), that displays the words "Arbeit Macht Frei", ("Work will make you free"), inscribed in iron. Auschwitz I is also the home of the State Museum that now administers Auschwitz. Barrack 24 was part of the Auschwitz I penal colony. The second section of Auschwitz, Auschwitz II, was the Birkenau death camp. Birkeneau's imposing entrance gate, with the ominous central guard tower and railroad tracks leading through the middle of it, straight into the crematoria, is perhaps the most iconic image of Nazi concentration camps. There were four crematoria at Birkeneau and up to 132,000 human beings, mostly Jews, were incinerated there each month after being killed in the gas chambers. The third part of the complex, called Auschwitz III, or Auschwitz Manowitz, was a slave labor camp where prisoners worked for the I.G. Farben Company, making chemicals and munitions.

Upon his arrival my father was sent to Birkeneau, the death camp.

After I stood waiting about three or four minutes in the anteroom another woman appeared, emerging from behind the file cabinets beyond the glass. She was middle-aged, a stocky brunette in a white business suit. She opened a door leading from the file room to the anteroom where I stood and she faced me. Her demeanor suggested she was busy and that I had interrupted her. Making brief eye contact and keeping the door open, she pointed to a pile of forms sitting on the table.

The forms were the same as the one I had already filled out. Without speaking she indicated that I should fill out a form, then promptly turned to return to the file room. I stopped her and said, "Please wait. Yes. I have that form. I filled it out. Here it is." I held up the form.

Continuing to say nothing, she let the door close slowly behind her and walked towards me. I held the form up for her to read. Assuming she did not speak English, for she had still not said a word to me, I pointed to the line on the form that said "Camp Number in KL Auschwitz", showing her my father's number, 124124.

Suddenly, she looked up at me, smiling somewhat sadly. I felt warmth. Certainly many researchers and scholars come to the archives at Auschwitz, and perhaps she mistook me for a professional researcher when she first approached me. But that shifted when she saw I was inquiring about my father, one of the few Jewish tattooed Auschwitz prisoners who had survived. She took the form from my hand, saying nothing but signaling for me to wait. She then walked back through the wooden door, into the file room. Through the window I could watch her. She walked slowly down the row of file cabinets with my form in her right hand, glancing up from my form to the file cabinets. Again and again she glanced from my form to the file cabinets.

The only document I possessed testifying to my father's time at Auschwitz was his original ID card from the Feldafing DP Camp where he was sent after the war to recover. It listed him as a "political prisoner...imprisoned in Auschwitz" during the war. As the Soviets closed in to liberate Auschwitz at the end of January 1945, the Nazis attempted to hide their crimes by hastily, and incompletely, exploding the death camp's gas chambers and crematoria. And they set about burning all prisoner records. The remnants of the gas chambers and crematoria remain, but most of the prisoner records were destroyed. The very few original prisoner records recovered at Auschwitz are among the rarest, most precious artifacts of the Holocaust.

Waiting and watching as the woman in white moved down the row of files, my lifetime of connection with Auschwitz stirred within me. I took a deep breath when I saw the woman in white pull a 5 x 7 index card out of a file cabinet. She had found something.

She looked at the index card in her left hand. She looked at the form I had filled out in her right. Checking it a second time, she again looked at the card in her left hand, and looked back at my form in the right. She closed the file drawer, turned around, and not looking at me went to a desk immediately behind her, picked up a phone and called someone. She read to that person from the index card and from the form I had filled out. They spoke for three or four minutes. Then the woman in white hung up the phone, put my form and the index card down on the desk next to the phone. She glanced towards me, said nothing, turned and walked back to the far end of the room, behind the file cabinets where I could not see her, to the area from which she had originally emerged. That was the last I saw of the woman in white.

Five minutes passed. The form I had filled out and the index card pulled from the files sat on the desk. I kept looking through the window into the room, not daring to turn away. I knew something was happening but no one was to be seen. The hip-looking young woman who had been typing when I first arrived was now gone. I stared into the room of file cabinets, saw no one and continued to wait, never turning my gaze away.

Suddenly, a door opened up that I hadn't noticed before, toward the rear of the file cabinet room. A slim, light haired woman in her mid-thirties walked directly to where the index card and my form sat. She studied them for about a minute, then took them and left through the same door from which she had entered.

Two or three minutes later she walked into the anteroom where I was standing. "Hello" she said, looking directly into my eyes. "I am Edyta Chowaniec, an archivist here at Auschwitz." "Hello" I said, returning her direct gaze. Holding up the form I had filled out with my father's information, she continued: "Please tell me, who are you in relation to this person?"

"I am his son." I said. "My name is Allen Hershkowitz."

"Ok" she said. "We have three files about your father. Please sit down"

There is much I do not know about my father and mother. Some of what I do know about their history, I think, is this: My father was a quiet, emotionally gentle and physically strong man. He was born on December 12, 1912, in Lubien, then a small, mercantile farming community in southwest Poland. My mother was a resourceful, intellectually oriented aesthete, and a classic east European Jewish cook. She was born Chasia Katz in Vilna into an affluent Orthodox Jewish family on December 22, 1915. Poland was at one time Europe's largest state, a "dual commonwealth"[2] comprised of land deriving from the Kingdom of Poland, which is where my father's town of Lubien is located, and land originating from the Grand Duchy of Lithuania, which is where my mother's town of Vilna is located. In 1922, seven years after my mother's birth, Lithuania became an independent state.

My father's family owned a small cattle farm and my father was a kosher butcher. His family's home and property were stolen by the Nazis and by Polish anti-

Semites during the war. He was never compensated. In the forty-five years that I knew him I never heard him raise his voice or swear. The only time he ever hit me—a swift, strong kick when I was about 10 years old—was an act instigated by my sister Suzanne, his unqualified favorite in our home. My sister was high-strung as a girl, but who could blame her? She was born only two years after my parents arrived in the United States. Complications arose during delivery and my mother was assisted in caring for my sister early in her life by another Holocaust survivor, Ann Jaffe, who we called Hannah. Hannah lived with her husband Ed near our building on St. Johns Place in Crown Heights, Brooklyn.

After liberation, my father met my mother at the Feldafing DP camp in Germany. She had been assigned to issue the permission slips to the meat butchers in the camp who slaughtered the cattle for inmate meals. My father was one of those butchers. Catching his eye, and because they each needed someone, my mother and father devised a scheme whereby she would issue him two calf-killing permits for every one she recorded. He butchered the unrecorded calf and sold it in the DP camp's black market. With the few proceeds they saved they fled on foot to France in 1946, to find my father's uncle, who lived in Rheims, about 90 miles northeast of Paris, where he settled around 1917 after leaving Poland to avoid military service in the first World War. They had to sneak in to France—"break the border" they called it—and among the few stories they both told me was the one of them traveling for days on foot to get into France, and my mother's exhaustion in doing so. Finally, not being able to travel any longer, my mother decided to give up and told my father that she could not go on. She sat on a downed tree and said, "Let me die here." That tree marked the border.

They had made it out of Germany. How they managed to find my father's uncle I do not know, but Rheims in those days was a lot less populated than it is today. In Rheims, my father worked in his uncle's laundry and my mother cleaned homes. In late 1947 or early 1948, they never clarified that precisely, they found out that the visas to the United States they had applied for were approved. How they found this out I do not know, but they did tell me that they had to pick up the visas in Bremen, Germany. Having no passports, only their Feldafing DP camp ID cards, which listed them as "stateless", they had to sneak back into Germany to obtain the visas. From documents I received as a result of my Auschwitz visit I learned that they were married in Bremen, Germany on January 9th, 1948— I had not previously known the date of my parents' wedding anniversary and it was never celebrated in my home—and shortly thereafter they were issued tickets for different dates of travel to New York City on a ship called the Marine Tiger.

According to records I obtained after my visit to Auschwitz from the International Tracing Service, my mother departed Bremen on January 12, 1948, three days after her marriage to my father.[3] She spent her "honeymoon" alone on the Marine Tiger headed for America. My father arrived in New York City in early February, and somehow he promptly found my mother, who had arrived two weeks earlier and was residing in a United Jewish Appeal domicile on the Upper West Side. When another female resident in the UJA house told her that "ihr mann" (your man) was downstairs, my mother thought she was being teased unkindly. She thought she'd never she him again.

They moved to Brooklyn—they were among the first religious Jews to populate the Crown Heights neighborhood after the war-- and my father immediately obtained work in a kosher butcher shop on Essex Street, in Manhattan's Lower East Side. "I arrived on a Friday and had a job on Monday" he told me. My sister and I were both born in Crown Heights—she in 1950 and me, numerous miscarriages later, in 1955. After a few years my father left Essex Street and opened his own butcher store in Brooklyn, on the corner of Brighton Beach Avenue and 5th Street, and when I was four years old we moved from Crown Heights to 764 East 91st Street in East Flatbush, directly across the street from Ditmas Park. When I was ten years old changing demographics demanding less kosher meat and the emergence of what were being called "supermarkets" put my father's small butcher store out of business, and he went to work in the meat markets on the lower west side of Manhattan. From the time I could first remember until I was twelve my father left for work every day at six AM and returned every night at eight, except on Fridays when he closed the store early for the Sabbath. On Saturdays he was home— we kept a kosher and observant household—but after a while our attendance at synagogue on Saturdays diminished. In 1967 my parents formed a partnership with another Holocaust survivor family and opened a Carvel ice cream store on Sunrise Highway in Lynbrook, Long Island. The hours were from 10 AM to 1 AM, seven days a week, and my parents made the 28 mile round trip from our home in Brooklyn to the Lynbrook store virtually every day for more than 15 years. We never took a family vacation.

My father was not a scholar. It was my mother who drilled into me the importance of an education. My father didn't teach me to drive or play ball, to swim or to shave. He did not teach me to knot a tie. He never once read me a bedtime story or tucked me in at night. And yet, he was far and away the most inspiring man I have ever known. For me as his son, and certainly in a larger historical context, he was truly a great man. His life, and the life of my mother as well, was a miraculous drama.

I sat down with Edyta at the wood table in the anteroom and I placed my father's talis, his prayer shawl, in its bag, on top of it. That shawl, which I had seen my father wear so often during Sabbath services, the High Holy Days, at my Bar Mitzvah, means much to me, and it was especially important for me to bring it to Auschwitz. I took out my notebook and Edyta placed the index card pulled from the files before her, on which numbers and words were written in pencil, including the dates 6/6/43, 18/1/45, my father's name, spelled Leon Hershovitz, and another date, 12/12/08. When Edyta started speaking to me, I turned my attention to what she was saying and I wrote notes. She was kind and her gentle tone, the way she looked straight into my eyes when speaking made it clear that she understood that she was providing me with sad but important information about not only one of the most important people in my life but about an historical figure, a survivor of Auschwitz.

Edyta began by again telling me that it was very rare to find records about Auschwitz inmates, that the Nazis had tried to destroy all records before abandoning the camp. Also, she said she would send me copies of the records they had about my father. It is from those records that she could tell me what I write below.

"Your father arrived here on June 6th, 1943. He was shipped to Auschwitz from Pomorze [Pomerania] in the north of Poland, where he was kept after his capture. There he was kept in a prison or in a ghetto for Jews. He lived in Auschwitz until January 18th or 19th 1945, and he was then forced into the Death March. The Nazis shipped the prisoners out on the Death March as the Soviets were arriving to liberate Auschwitz."

I had heard of the Death March before Edyta mentioned it, but I never imagined that my father was part of it. Of the 1.1 million Jews who entered Auschwitz, only about 56,000 remained alive as the Soviets approached to liberate the camp in January 1945. Most of the prisoners were forced into a four-day Death March, during which 20,000 of them were murdered: those who sought rest, those who needed to relieve themselves at an inopportune time, those who tried to flee, those too weak to pull the handcarts containing the luggage of the SS--all were shot or beaten to death along the March. My father had arrived at Auschwitz in June 1943 and had spent more than a year and a half—19 months--in the camp under horrific circumstances; I cannot imagine what condition my father was in on January 18th or 19th 1945 when he was forced into the Death March.

Edyta told me that my father's Death March journey took him from Auschwitz to the Gross-Rosen concentration camp. I had known nothing about this. During the afternoon of January 18th or 19th the BIIB barrack (B-2-B) in Auschwitz, where my father resided, was ordered into formation and the prisoners departed on foot in the direction of Gliwice (Gleiwitz). According to Edyta, "It was minus twenty degrees Celsius when he left Auschwitz and he was force-marched for almost four days to either the town of Pszczyna or the town of Gliwice. From one of those towns he was put into a freight car and shipped to the Gross-Rosen concentration camp, located in what is now the Czech Republic." Food was virtually non-existent. My father would have been given either a single loaf of bread or a few slices of cheese, gleaned from leftover food in the Auschwitz kitchen, for the journey. He was given no blanket, no additional clothes or intact shoes. At the end of the Death March, underdressed, nearly barefoot, starving, stiff, damp and freezing from the cold and the snow, my father was sent to Gross-Rosen. The route of the Auschwitz Death March has been documented largely by memorials, along the route, to the thousands of prisoners murdered along the Death March, just before what would have been their liberation.

As a boy, the only nights I ate dinner with my father at the small pink Formica kitchen table in our home was on a Friday or a Saturday, when his butcher shop was closed, or on a Sunday, when the store closed early. On one of those nights, in 1966, when I was eleven years old, as we watched a Huntley-Brinkley Report newscast on NBC showing dead soldiers in Vietnam, back when the military had not yet learned to visually shield Americans from the horrors of war and allowed cameras on the battlefield, my father spoke at dinner, which he rarely did. Looking at the TV and then turning to me he said: "I'm sorry Sonny, to tell you this." "Sonny" and "Butch" were his terms of endearment for me. "I'm sorry to tell you this, but I sat on dead people."

Apparently, seeing the bodies of US soldiers on TV, and knowing I was watching that carnage right there with him, he felt he could share something he had to express, offering information he never spoke about. He didn't elaborate. At the time, I knew my parents were survivors of concentration camps; I had a vague notion that they were previously married and had children who were murdered. But I did not know the names of any of those earlier families, I did not know where my parents were born, how much schooling they had, how many brothers and sisters they had, how those family members died. And I feared that asking would open their wounds. I craved any information at all from my parents about their past, so I saw no reason for my father's apology. But in retrospect, having raised three children of my own, I understand his well-mannered need to apologize for this gruesome admission. He revealed nothing further. I now assume it was probably in the course of the Death March or in the freight car to Gross-Rosen that his sitting on dead people occurred.

Edyta continued: "As the Soviets were coming to liberate Gross-Rosen, in mid-February 1945, your father was then placed in another freight car and transferred to the Dachau concentration camp. His Dachau prisoner registration number was 140132."

My father was also a survivor of the Dachau? I of course knew that my mother was imprisoned there. I was told she survived, or rather was kept alive, as part of the Dachau medical experiments. But my father? Of course, my mother never told me about the experiments. I learned that from a cousin named Betty Ballin (nee Krenik), one of my very few cousins, the daughter of my father's French uncle. She was a young girl in Rheims when my parents arrived and was among the first to meet my parents after liberation. Cousin Betty mentioned matter-of-factly, that my mother was part of medical experiments at Dachau, during a dinner I shared with her one night when I was seventeen years old at her home in Manhasset, on Long Island. I was stunned.

At that same dinner Betty also told me that my mother's daughter—whose name I do not know to this day: I could never bring myself to ask-- and my mother's mother were murdered in Dachau. Betty explained that upon arrival at Dachau the Nazis immediately sent mothers with their children to their death. Seeking to save my mother, *her* mother, my grandmother, took my mother's daughter upon their arrival and claimed she was her own, whereupon she and my mother's daughter were sent to die. This is how my grandmother saved my mother's life. My mother's first husband, her father and five or six brothers and sisters (I am still not clear on how many she had) were killed before she arrived at concentration camp from the Vilna ghetto.

But based on information I obtained after my visit to Auschwitz from the International Tracing Service (ITS) about my mother, it is likely that Betty was wrong about the location of the murder of my mother's daughter and my grandmother, and also about the location of the medical experiments. From information the ITS sent me in October 2012, I learned that the first concentration camp my mother went to after her internment in the Vilna ghetto was not Dachau, but the Stutthof death camp. According to ITS records, she was sent there on September 6th, 1941 and remained there for just about three full years, until August 14th, 1944, when she was transferred to Dachau. Stutthof was the first Nazi death camp built outside of Germany, completed on September 2, 1939. It is located west of the Polish town of Sztutowo, (Stutthof in German), 21 miles east of Gdansk, Poland. It was the last camp to be liberated by the Allies and was a particularly barbaric place where small-scale production of soap produced from the remains of murdered Jewish victims took place. If my mother's daughter was separated from her after the Vilna ghetto, it is likely to have occurred here. The murder of my mother's daughter and mother in Stutthof might explain why the name of that camp was never uttered in my home. Until just a few months ago, I had no idea that my mother was a prisoner there, much less a prisoner there for three years. As for my mother's being part of medical experiments, to my knowledge everyone experimented on at Dachau died during the procedures. If she was indeed part of medical experiments, it is more likely that they were the activities at Stutthof, which did not always result in the death of the victim. According to one Stutthof survivor, Maria Haluschkewych, Nazi SS commanders forced her "to hold the heads of Jewish parents steady so they would see their children mutilated in so-called medical experiments...{she] would have been shot had she refused."[4]

I have never allowed myself to contemplate details related to Betty's allegations that the Nazis experimented on my mother, but knowing that Nazis experimented on my mother was even a possibility is an indescribable sadness that I have carried since I was a teenager.

One of the documents contained in my father's Auschwitz file is titled "Zugang von Gross-Rosen (Auschwitz) auf 28.1.45," which means "Departure from Gross-Rosen on January 28, 1945." It is a list of prisoners who arrived at Gross-Rosen from Auschwitz and who were packed into a freight car and shipped to Dachau on January 28, 1945. Even while retreating from approaching Soviet forces, the Nazis were still obsessed with keeping records of the Jews they intended to kill, to assure that none escaped their grasp.

I was told as a child by my parents that they met in the Feldafing DP camp in Germany after the war. Feldafing was a recovery facility for concentration camp survivors. I have in my dining room in a frame my father's original Feldafing ID card, dated 20.3.46, which indicates he was a "political prisoner" in Auschwitz. It lists his nationality as "stateless." It lists my father's date of birth as 12.12.12, which is what he told me it was, and spells his surname as Herszkowicz. I always wondered how it was that my father got to Feldafing, located in Germany and far away from Auschwitz, which is in Poland. Now I knew. He was shipped to Feldafing from Dachau.

The Americans liberated Dachau, and the Americans administered Feldafing. The Soviets liberated Auschwitz and Gross-Rosen. Being liberated by the Americans allowed my parents to emigrate to the West--first to France, then to the United States. Otherwise my father would have been forced to stay in communist Poland, Czechoslovakia, or East Germany. "Your father had big luck," Edyta told me. In a way, I guess he did, putting aside the murder of his children and wife, his parents and siblings, and his years in prison, and the almost twenty months— including two winters—he spent in Auschwitz, as well as the Death March and imprisonment in Gross-Rosen and Dachau.

Edyta paused and furrowed her brow. She looked at me seriously, spoke deliberately and said this: "Something is not clear to me. Seventy-five percent of the people who were sent to Auschwitz were selected to be killed right away. Of the twenty-five percent chosen for forced labor, like your father, most died within six or seven months. I heard of one prisoner who lived nine months and another who lived a year. But your father lived here for more than 18 months. I never heard of anyone living for so long in Auschwitz. It was impossible to survive in Auschwitz for almost two years using only camp food. He had to find something else to eat."

"He did." I said. "He told me that he found a way to steal food from the guard dogs." Taking out a small map of Auschwitz-Birkeneau, Edyta said, "OK, here is where they kept the dogs". She pointed to a location at the southeastern section of the death camp. "He must have worked around here. That would have given him access to steal the dog food."

Did he steal dog food every day? That is a historical question about my father that I just can't bring myself to contemplate for too long. Still, it is remarkable that he lived. As Primo Levi wrote: "at Auschwitz, in 1944, of the old Jewish prisoners...[those with] low numbers less than 150,000, only a few hundred had survived."[5] My father had a low number: 124124.

Edyta continued, "When he arrived your father was unloaded from a freight car here." She pointed to tracks on the Auschwitz map located at the western side of Birkeneau. He arrived before the main tracks were laid through the center of the entry gate. "Your father came here at a very good time, in summer, that made it easier for him to survive. Still, in the summer, the prisoners had to work twelve or more hours each day. In the winter a little less. After being unloaded and selected for work on June 6th, [1943] he was sent to barrack B1B." [B-one-B] She showed me on her map of the camp where that barrack was. She continued: "Then, in July '43, one month later, he was transferred to Barrack BIIB, [B-two-B] near the gypsy barracks, and near the crematoria," and she showed me on a map where that barrack was as well.

The gas chambers murdered groups of up to 2,000 people at a time, and many groups were murdered each day. Then the bodies were carried by Jewish slave laborers to the adjacent crematoria. My father told me he was often near the crematoria. During my visit to the site where his wooden prisoner barrack once stood I could see the crematoria less than 100 yards away. He must have smelled the bodies burning. He must have heard the screams of the innocents being gassed.

He told me that one night he was forced to sleep outside the crematoria. He was the first on a line of prisoners scheduled to be gassed the next day. In the morning, a Nazi guard came to the front of the line and said, "We need five workers. You, you, you, you and you, come with me." My father was the first on line, the first man the guard selected for work. He was spared the gas chamber.

"I built Birkeneau," my father told me more than once. Edyta thinks he was involved in the building of the wooden barracks as Birkeneau was being expanded. My father told me he was saved in part by "having an outside job." Given the proximity of the main gate to the location where the dogs were kept, and given the fact that that entry gate was expanded at the end of 1943, when my father was there, it is likely he was among those slave laborers who built that famous, emblematic entrance to Birkeneau.

After about an hour of listening to Edyta's information I closed my notebook and stood up. We quietly exchanged contact information. I held her hand in both of mine and she assured me again that copies of the original documents related to my father's incarceration would be sent to me. I left Edyta and the archivist's office in Auschwitz I. I walked first to a small gallows and then to the shooting wall, places where prisoners were routinely hung and shot for minor infractions of camp rules. I put on my father's talis and the yarmulke from my bar mitzvah. I touched the shooting wall with both of my hands and said a prayer. From Auschwitz I I went to the grounds of Birkeneau. I went first to the camp's western train tracks and stopped at a freight car sitting at the location where my father was unloaded when he first arrived. I put both my hands on it, closed my eyes and wept. I then walked into the camp. There were others walking the grounds, a group of Japanese students, a film crew, a group of young Europeans here and there. No one looked at each other in the eye, or at least no one looked me in the eye, perhaps out of respect for the tears on my face. I walked up the train tracks leading toward the site of my father's barrack, near the gas chambers and crematoria.

Suddenly, I panicked. I had forgotten to ask Where on the premises was he tattooed? Where did the Nazis put the numbers on my father's arm? I had to know that. I had to go to that place.

I called Edyta on my cell phone from the grounds of Birkeneau. "Where are you standing?" she asked when I asked my question. I said, "I am standing on the central train tracks leading to the crematoria. I am near the place of my father's barrack, facing the gas chambers." She said, "OK. Look to your left. Do you see the three brick buildings?" I responded, "Yes, I do." "The one in the back," she said, "that building was a washroom. That is where your father was tattooed with his numbers."

I paused, looking at the building about 500 yards from the central train tracks, where I stood. I thought about how I worshipped my father when I was a boy, and how his silence intimidated and saddened me; how it created a distance between us that I wanted so badly to bridge. I recalled how I often proclaimed as a young boy that I wanted to be a butcher, like him, and how he would laugh with pride whenever I said that. It was among the few times that I saw him laugh. I recalled how we once played catch, only once, and once played soccer, only once, before anyone was playing soccer in New York City and at which he seemed capable. I recalled how those were the only times we played sports together. I remembered the one movie we went to together, The Sound of Music, with my mother, in 1965, when I was ten years old. I felt sad that we didn't share more activities together because he was always working. And I thought about the tattooed numbers on his arm.

I studied the washroom building from afar. The building seemed so small. It was narrow and dark. I tried to visualize the moment he was tattooed. What did he think was happening? How distraught, how frightened was he? What did he look like? What was going through his mind? Certainly he knew of the Old Testament prohibition against being tattooed, the reason Jews traditionally do not have tattoos. By the time he entered the washroom his children and his wife were already murdered. His parents and five or six brothers and sisters were also murdered. Did he expect to survive? He couldn't possibly know anything about the barbarity of the Birkeneau death camp he was about to experience--the gas chambers, the crematoria. How *did* he survive? Why did he want to?

When I was 25 years old, in 1980, I decided to convert my father's tattoo from an expression of evil violation into a memorial of triumph. I was teaching a summer course at Brooklyn College at the time and one of my students wore a short sleeve shirt revealing a large tattoo of an open winged eagle on his arm. I asked him where I could get a tattoo and he told me about a New York City fireman who lived in Park Slope, Brooklyn, who did tattooing to earn spare cash. I went to visit the fireman and told him to tattoo my arm. At first, I considered having him tattoo the same numbers on my arm that the Nazis forced onto my father's arm. I read recently that getting tattoos of the numbers is now a fad in Israel among grandchildren of Holocaust survivors. However, as I sat on the chair ready to receive my father's numbers, I changed my mind. I decided that a better way to prevail over the Nazis' desecration of my father's body was to transform his numbers into a flower. I chose a rose, my mother's favorite. I had it placed high on my arm, so it could not be seen even if I wore a short sleeve shirt.

On November 4th, 2011, one month after my visit, just as Edyta had promised, I received an email from Piotr Supiński of the Auschwitz Office For Information On Former Prisoners. Attached to the email were copies of three documents, one of which was the Auschwitz induction form containing the information gathered by Nazi interrogators upon my father's arrival at the camp.

The Auschwitz induction form was one page, filled-in in the handwriting of the Nazi guard who interrogated and physically evaluated my father after he made it through the initial immediate-death or slave-labor selection. Who was the interrogator who made this momentous choice? How old was he? Is he dead now? Did he work alone or was there a team of Nazis evaluating my father? How did he treat my father? What condition was my father in while he went through this ordeal? He had just gotten out of a freight car from his prison in the north of Poland.

The induction form is titled "Konzentrationslager Auschwitz" and the header line at the top asks "Reason for Imprisonment" (Art den Haft) to which the Nazi interrogator provides the following straightforward answer: "Yude", (Jew). Immediately to the right of that is indicated the number that was tattooed onto my father's left arm: 124124.

Under the header of the Auschwitz induction form the first line lists my father's name as Herszkowicz Laizer Israel. This spelling of my father's name is different than his name as I knew it, Leon Hershkowitz, the name he ultimately came to have after his processing at Auschwitz, Gross-Rosen, Dachau and Feldafing. It's the name he brought with him to the United States in 1948. Moreover, his middle name was not Israel: Beginning sometime at the end of 1938 the Nazis started to require every

Jewish person to adopt a middle name that would distinguish him or her as a Jew. The Nazis mandated that all women take on the middle name of Sarah, and that all Jewish men take the middle name of Israel. What his true middle name was, or if he even had one, I will never know.

On the induction form my father's birth date is listed as 12.12.08, not the 12.12.12 I know it to be. His birthplace is listed as Lubien, as is his pre-capture residence. Lubien (pronounced "Lube Yen") is in southwest Poland, near the German border. On the small cattle farm that he and his family owned, my father worked as a butcher, and on his Auschwitz interrogation form his vocation is listed as "worker." (His Gross-Rosen transport listing describes his vocation as "fleischer," or butcher.) His nationality is listed as "former Poland". Being a Polish Jew was the worst combination when it came to the Nazi's agenda.

The fifth line of the Auschwitz induction form asks my father's nationality, and the sixth line inquires as to the name of my father's parents, which is recorded as Yojna and Rifka. That line also records my grandmother's maiden name, Krejnik. (My middle name, Joel, is derived from my grandfather's name, and my sister's middle name, Regina, is the name of my maternal grandmother.)

Then the form inquires about my grandmother's and grandfather's "race", which is listed as "jud", jew.

Race. Jew. As I translate this line of the form I stop, sigh, and take a long pause. I dwell on the words "Race" and "Jew." Is there a more divisive word in the English language than Race? "Race is an utter fiction," writes Wade Davies. "We are all cut from the same genetic cloth."

The eighth line on the Auschwitz form asks the habitation of my father's parents and the line on the form is filled in with two abbreviations in German that I can only assume means they are dead, or their whereabouts are unknown.

The ninth line on the form asks the name of my father's wife, not my mother, but his first wife, who was killed with his younger son at their home in Lubien when the Germans first invaded. From this form I learn that her name was Cypre, a name never uttered in my home. I vividly remember the shock, the visceral blow I felt in my belly as a boy when I learned that my father had a previous wife, and my mother a previous husband, and how I felt I had to bear that information alone. It could not be discussed. Not even my sister and I spoke about it. Under the name Cypre, line nine asks where she resides, and, as with my father's parents, it indicates either that she is dead, or her whereabouts are unknown.

My father told me "The war started on Sunday and I was captured on Monday." He was close. It must have seemed that he was captured on the second day of the war given the proximity of Lubien to the German border. But September 1st, 1939, the day Germany invaded western Poland, was a Friday. When the Germans first invaded, my father was not at home. Upon his return he found his wife Cypre murdered, along with his sister and his younger child. I recall my father telling me that his younger child was a two-year-old boy, but I never learned his name. My sister thought this child was a girl. His older child, a five year old son named Heinich, was still alive, but he was not alive for long: as my father tried to escape with him, the boy was shot. According to what my father told me, his last word was "Tata", which means Daddy in Yiddish. According to my sister, my father told her that Heinich's last words were "Don't worry daddy, they won't get you." After my father was captured in early September 1939, he was sent north to the town of Pomorze, to a prison, from which he was later sent to Auschwitz in 1943. I did not know of his incarceration at Pomorze until Edyta provided me with this information from his Auschwitz file.

The tenth line on the Auschwitz form asks how many children my father has, or had, and it indicates two. He told me he had two sons, but he could not bring himself ever to discuss them.

Line eleven of the Auschwitz induction form asks about my father's educational background. It indicates that he attained the 4th level of school. My mother's family included rabbis and other scholars, and she was raised in an urban, intellectual environment. She completed gymnasium—the equivalent of high school—while my father's only education was perhaps some years at heder. My father was an ethical, hard working polyglot. He loved to tinker with repairs around our home. He liked to paint our outside porch. But he worked so much, five and a half days each week at the butcher store, seven days a week at the Carvel ice cream store, and for very long hours at both places, that he also liked to rest. He was not intellectually cultured, as my mother was, and their different origins sometimes caused tension as they grew older. However little money my family had, and we had little, my mother would nevertheless say "There is always money for books." My father, by contrast, would wonder why I needed to buy another book when I already had so many on my shelves.

The next section of the Auschwitz induction form is macabre. Entry spaces include the following physical attributes described by the Nazi evaluating my father: height (167 cm); nose ("straight"); hair ("brown"); build (not decipherable...); mouth ("normal"); beard ("none"); appearance ("slim"); ears ("medium size"); eyebrows ("brown"); teeth ("good").

The form also inquires as to the language he spoke (Polish and German), whether he had any infectious diseases (no), was a pension recipient (no) or, strangely, whether he had a special license plate (no).

The last questions on the form inquire whether my father was involved in any political organizations, (he wasn't), and whether he had any criminal or "political convictions", (he didn't).

The bottom of the Auschwitz induction form ends with the following statement, requiring my father's signature:

"It has been pointed out to me that my punishment will be due to the intellectual forgery of documents, if the aforementioned documents are proven to be false." My father's signature then follows.

During 1973 and 1974, Elie Wiesel launched his influential seminar "The Holocaust as Literature" at City College, his first academic home. This was twelve years before he was awarded the Nobel Peace Prize, and I was one of his first students. On April 9th, 2008, during a speech Elie delivered at City when he was awarded an honorary Doctor of Letters degree, he recounted a conversation we had when I was his student. According to the City College transcript of that speech, Elie said:

"One day one of my students, a sensitive young man who was eager to learn, came to my office and began weeping. When he stopped weeping he said: 'my father was married and his wife and children perished during the Holocaust; and my mother was married and her husband and child also perished. My parents met after World War II in a Displaced Persons Camp and they had me. But I know that whenever they see me they don't only see me.' That is why he wept."[6]

I remember that conversation well. It was the first time I ever shared feelings about my parents' history with anyone. The conversation took place while Elie and I discussed the essay I was required to write for his seminar, in which I imagined what my father might have felt and thought when I first asked him why he had numbers tattooed on his arm.

Elie Wiesel's philosophy, that it is life that ultimately shows us the way, is true. And yet, suffering is the part of life that guides us to wisdom. From the time I learned that my parents had three children murdered, I knew that I would have three children, to replace them, that I would make another attempt to sooth their wounds. That I would bring back what the Nazis took away. And I did. So there was no greater joy for me than to bring my parents together with my kids. For 25 years I have had photos hanging on my office wall of my father pitching a baseball to my oldest son, something he never did with me, and my mother happily cooking with my daughter and hugging my youngest son, when my kids were young. I view those photos as much more than photos of grandparents with their grandchildren. They are much more: they confirm my family's triumph over the Nazis.

The word "Perseverance" is etched into the top of each of my parents' gravestones. My mother, Helen Hershkowitz, died on July 1st, 1994, in St. Vincent hospital in New York City's Greenwich Village. She was seventy-eight. As she lay dying, I asked that she help take care of my children from wherever she was going. "I'll do my best," she said. Those were her last words to me. My father, Leon Hershkowitz, lived on for six years without her, then passed away on October 20th, 2000, at the age of 87 in Delray Beach, Florida. The last words he said to me, after I told him that I loved him while he lay in his hospital bed, were words I had never heard him utter before: "Yeah Sonny, Ok, I love you too."

****

Endnotes

1. Primo Levi, Survival in Auschwitz, (New York, Touchstone, 1958) at pp. 27-28
2. Norman Davies, "Poland: Malice, Death, Survival", New York Review of Books, January 10, 2013, pp 47 &48
3. According to my mother's decomposing Marine Tiger passenger ticket, which I discovered buried within my sister's family files

after her death in 2018, the ship was "set to sail" on January 13th, 1948, not January 12th.

4. http://www.catholicsentinel.org/main.asp?
SectionID
=2&SubSectionID=35&ArticleID=9156

5. Levi, Survival, p. 89

6. The City College of New York, "Alumnus",
Summer 2008, at p 4

Edyta Chowaniec, Archivist,
Auschwitz Birkenau State
Museum, Oswiecim, Poland.
Photo by J. Henry Fair,
October 3, 2011

Printed in the USA
CPSIA information can be obtained
at www.ICGtesting.com
LVHW020931071024
793120LV00040B/752